when I was a
ring bearer

Designer Iona Hoyle
Commissioning Editor Annabel Morgan
Production Toby Marshall
Picture research Emily Westlake
Art Director Leslie Harrington
Publishing Director Alison Starling

First published in 2009 by
Ryland Peters & Small
20–21 Jockey's Fields
London WC1R 4BW
and
519 Broadway, Fifth Floor
New York, NY 10022
www.rylandpeters.com

10 9 8 7 6 5 4 3 2 1

Text, design, and commissioned
photography © Ryland Peters & Small
2009

Printed in China

ISBN 978 1 84597 921 8

when I was a
ring bearer

Leigh Crandall

RYLAND
PETERS
& SMALL

LONDON NEW YORK

when I was a ring bearer

This book belongs to Charlie Garner. I live at 403 N 7th Girard, Il and am 4 years old. I was the ring bearer at the wedding of

Hannah Roberts and Nick Graham, which was held at Overlook Farms Clarksville Mo on August 6, 2011 at 5:00 pm

I know the bride and groom because I am Hannah's nephew

paste a photo of you with
the bride and groom here

congratulations!

If you're reading this you've probably been asked to be the ring bearer in a wedding—a very exciting and important job.

So, first things first. What's this book for? Well, it's for a few different things. The first is to help you understand what being a ring bearer is all about. You'll find pages explaining who's who at the wedding, what your role is, and what will happen on the wedding day.

The second thing is to help you remember the day. There are lots of places where you can write about your experience of being a ringbearer—they'll be funny to read over when you're older.

The third and most important thing is to have fun! There's a game to play, lots of space to draw or stick in pictures, and even a few crazy dance moves for you to try. There's also room for any notes from the new friends you'll make.

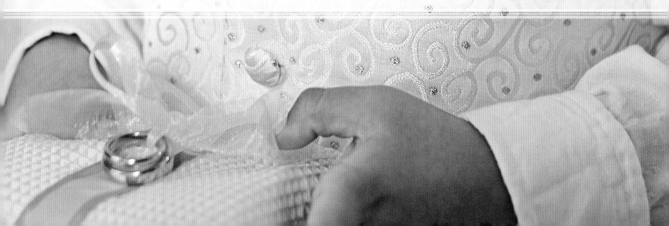

Preparations

being a ring bearer

It's a great honor to be asked to be a ring bearer. It means you're very special to the bride and groom, and they trust you to play an important role in their big day! As a ring bearer you're a member of the wedding party, which is the name for the group of people who take part in the wedding ceremony. Sometimes there is just one ring bearer (that's you!) but other times there may be another boy around your age who serves as a ring bearer with you. It may be your brother, a cousin, or someone else you know already.

Your main job will be carrying the ring pillow down the aisle during the ceremony. This is a pretty cushion with the two wedding rings tied on with ribbon or braid. Sometimes the rings on the pillow will be real, but more often they are just pretend ones, and the best man has the real ones safe in his pocket. That's good, because you won't have to worry about losing them. You'll also be one of the groom's helpers, pose for a lot of photos, and get to go to a cool party!

who's who
and what they do

the bride and groom

A wedding is all about celebrating the marriage of these two people. They'll be very excited and probably also a little nervous on the day of the wedding, so be as helpful as you can and be sure to offer them a hug and say, "congratulations!"

the best man

The best man is the groom's best friend or a close relative and will help the groom get ready on the wedding day. He'll stand next to the groom during the ceremony. The best man may also make a nice speech about the groom at the reception.

the best man was

....

the parents of the bride and groom

The bride and groom's family members sometimes walk down the aisle at the beginning of the ceremony. The bride's father will usually wait and walk her down the aisle last.

the family members were
Mommy - bridesmaid
Daddy - Walked Mama down the
asile

the ushers

The ushers are friends and relatives of the bride and the groom. They help guests find their seats before the ceremony, and may escort family members down the aisle.

the ushers were

....

....

....

13

the groomsmen

As a ring bearer, you are one of the guys in the wedding party and will get to hang out with the groom and all his groomsmen. Cool! The groomsmen are the groom's best friends and favorite relatives. They help the groom get ready on the wedding day and they stand up next to him during the ceremony. You may get ready with the groomsmen, travel to the ceremony together, and take lots of photos all together. If you have any questions on the wedding day, the groomsmen are good people to ask.

the groomsmen were

....

....

....

....

....

I had the most fun when

....

....

....

paste a photo of you with
the groom and groomsmen here

attendants

maid or matron of honor

The maid of honor (called the matron of honor if she is married) is the bride's best friend or a close relative, like her sister. She's the bride's main helper throughout the wedding day, and has the important job of making sure the bride's dress looks perfect before she walks down the aisle. During the wedding ceremony, the maid of honor stands near the bride and holds her bouquet. She may make a speech at the reception, talking about the bride.

the maid or matron of honor was

....

bridesmaids

These ladies are the bride's best friends and relatives. Their job is to help the bride on the day of the wedding. They'll walk down the aisle just before you do.

the bridesmaids were

....

....

flower girl

There can be one or more flower girls and they'll probably be around your age. Like you, they'll be dressed up in fancy clothes—pretty dresses, and maybe flowers in their hair. Their job is to throw flower petals as they walk down the aisle and to look very cute!

the flower girl(s) was

....

autographs

During the wedding reception, you can ask all the members of the wedding party to sign these pages. Your new friends can write their email addresses too, so you can keep in touch and maybe send each other your photos of the wedding!

rehearsal

There's an old saying that "practice makes perfect," so to make sure everything goes as well as possible during the actual wedding ceremony, you may have to go to a rehearsal (which just means a practice) at the ceremony location the day before the wedding.

This is good, because you'll get to meet all the other people in the wedding (if you haven't already). You'll also hear exactly what you have to do, which will be helpful on the wedding day. Each person will practice their part in the ceremony, including you! An adult will tell you when it's your turn to walk down the aisle and where to go once you get to the end. If you have any questions, go ahead and ask—this is the right time for figuring things out. Once the rehearsal is over, there's usually a dinner for everyone in the wedding party. Then it's off to bed to get a good night's sleep before the big day!

the wedding rehearsal was held at ....

I practiced ....

After we were finished with the rehearsal, we went to

....

I sat with ....

The best part of the rehearsal was ....

....

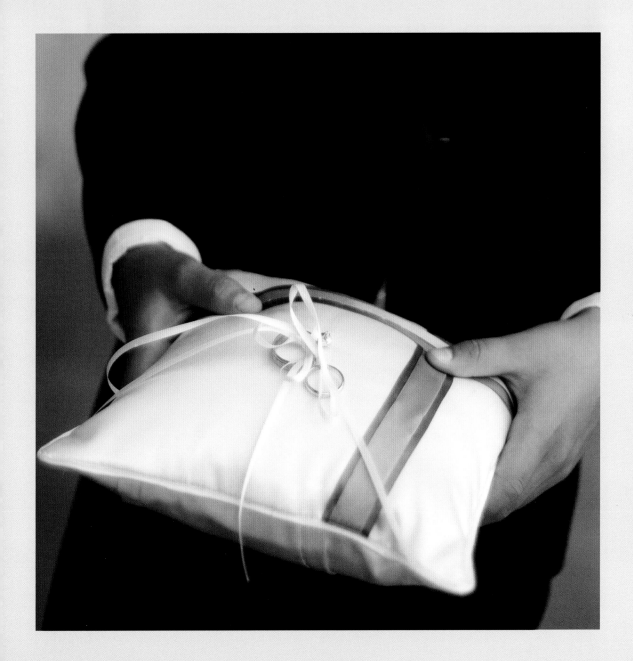

my outfit

The bride usually picks out the ring bearer's outfit, and you'll probably be dressed similarly to the other guys in the wedding party. You may have to go to a special store to buy your wedding clothes. Depending on how fancy the wedding is, you could be wearing pants and a nice shirt or even a tuxedo with a bow tie. On the wedding day, you'll want to hold off getting dressed until you're close to leaving for the ceremony. That way you won't have to worry about your clothes getting rumpled or dirty beforehand. Dress-up clothes aren't always the most comfortable, but it's important to look your best during the ceremony and for the photos afterwards. You'll be able to take off your tie and jacket later on at the reception.

paste a picture of you
in your outfit here

The Wedding Day

getting there

Since wedding days are special, the bride and groom will often rent a special kind of car to get themselves and the wedding party to the ceremony and the reception. And since you're a member of the wedding party, one type of car you might get to ride in is a called a limousine. These are long cars that are most often black or white. They usually have dark windows. Some have roofs that can open up, and even televisions inside! Some limousines are really big and can fit up to twenty people. Trolleys and buses might also be used if all of the guests need to get from one place to another after the ceremony has taken place.

The bride and groom usually rent a separate car for themselves. They might get a limo too, or they might get another type of fancy car. If the reception isn't too far away, they might skip the car and take a horse-drawn carriage instead.

I rode in a ....

the bride and groom rode in a ....

the ceremony

Wedding ceremonies can be held in many places. Some take place in churches or synagogues, some in hotels, and some outdoors. There have even been some underwater! No matter where the ceremony is, you will have practiced what to do during the rehearsal. You may walk down the aisle with another ring bearer, beside a flower girl, or on your own. Either the bridesmaids or the bride and her father will be following right behind you.

Once you're at the end of the aisle you'll be able to take a seat. The rings on the pillow probably won't be the actual ones the bride and groom use. This doesn't make carrying them any less important, but if the rings aren't real you'll keep the pillow when you sit down. If you're carrying the real wedding rings, you'll hand the pillow to the best man before you sit. At the end of the ceremony you'll walk back down the aisle behind the bride and groom. Your job is done and it's time to party!

feeling nervous

At the ceremony there may be a lot of guests, and it can feel a little scary to have so many people looking at you. It's normal to feel a little nervous, and if you start to get butterflies in your stomach, remember that you are surrounded by family and friends who love you. As you walk down the aisle, a good tip is to keep your eyes focused on the groom and the groomsmen who will be at the end of the aisle smiling and cheering you on. You can also try the trick of picturing everyone in funny hats, which makes the moment feel a little less serious! It might feel like everyone is looking at you, but don't forget that as soon as the bride appears in her beautiful dress, all eyes will be on her instead!

photographs from the ceremony

the reception

The reception is the party that's held after the
ceremony. It's the fun bit after the serious part of
getting married, and when the bride and groom get
to celebrate with all of their guests. There will be
speeches (they're called "toasts" at a wedding),
laughing, dinner, and dancing. The bride and groom
will cut their wedding cake, and pieces will be
passed around for everyone to get a taste. Yummy!
Receptions often go late into the evening, so you
may not get to stay until the very end, but you'll
still have plenty of time to hang out and hear
what a great job you did at the ceremony.

At the reception I sat with

....

I had the most fun talking to

....

We ate

....

....for dinner.

The cake flavor was

....

....and

....made toasts.

My favorite songs played were

....

....

bust a move

Once dinner is done it's time to hit the dance floor! Here are a few classic moves to try:

robot The idea here is to look like you're motorized. Keep your arms bent and locked in position and your legs in one spot, then move your upper body around.

fishing pole

Pretend you have a fishing pole in your hand. Cast out your line and then reel it back in to the beat of the music. Get someone else to pretend to be the fish and have them dance toward you as if you've caught them on your hook.

shopping cart

Keep your hands out in front of you and walk forward to the beat of the music, just as if you're pushing an imaginary shopping cart. Every few steps, stick an arm out and pretend you're grabbing a can off a shelf and putting it into your cart.

double dutch

You'll need two other people for this dance. They stand a few feet across from each other and pretend to turn two jump ropes around. You jump into the middle and pretend to jump over the ropes to the beat of the music. Take turns being in the middle.

*paste a photo or a picture
of yourself dancing here*

paste a photo of the wedding cake or your
favorite moment from the reception here

reception scavenger hunt

If things get a little boring at the reception (and you get tired of everyone telling you how cute you look in your outfit!), take a break and see if you can do all of the things below by the end of the reception.

- ✴ Count how many tables there are at the reception

- ✴ Find out what town the best man lives in

- ✴ Count the number of people wearing striped ties

- ✴ Ask the maid of honor what her favorite color is

- ✴ Find one person or thing at the reception that begins with each letter of the alphabet

- ✴ Do a funny dance

- ✴ Take a picture with a new friend you've met at the wedding

- ✴ Try a bite of food you've never tasted before

- ✴ Count the number of people wearing blue dresses

- ✴ Find out where the bride and groom are going for their honeymoon

- ✴ Tell the bride how pretty she looks

- ✴ Find three things from the reception to save in this book (some ideas are: a paper napkin, your place card, a flower from the arrangements at your table)

- ✴ Count how many people are on the dance floor during one song

photographs from the reception

happy memories

All this wedding stuff is a lot of fun, but it can be tiring too. You might want to sleep in for a while the day after the wedding, and then after you say your goodbyes you'll be on your way home. If you have a long drive or have to fly on a plane, use the time to fill in any blanks left in this book while you still remember everything clearly (you'll be glad you did!). You can also write the bride and groom a note or draw them a picture of their wedding as a thank you for having you as a part of it.

What I liked best about being a ring bearer was

....

....

My favorite part of the day was

....

....

My new friends from the wedding are

....

....

souvenirs from the big day

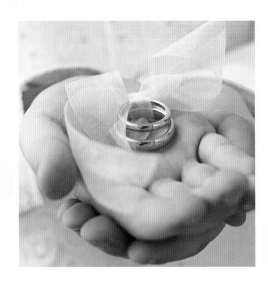

picture credits

Image on pages 42–43, 46–47 and endpapers are taken from *Japanese Patterns*, published by The Pepin Press (www.pepinpress.com)

All photography by Tara Fisher unless stated below:

Caroline Arber: page 12 below left; David Loftus: page 38 below left; Julie Mikos © Julie Mikos Photography www.juliemikos.com: pages 7 above left, 7 below right, 21, and 26; Polly Wreford: pages 16, 17 above left, 17 below right 20, 34, 36 below right background, 38 above both, 40, 41 above right, 41 below left, 44, 45 below, and 48 background; Viv Yeo: page 13 above right.

Ryland Peters & Small would like to thank the wonderful models photographed for this book: Bella, Kai, Rafferty, Barnaby, Jade and Mark.